Becoming Her The Proverbs 31 Woman

JANAI IMANI

Acknowledgments

First and foremost, I want to thank God for placing this devotional on my heart and guiding me through every step of its creation. Without His grace, this book would not exist.

To my incredible mother – thank you for being my editor, my encourager, and my greatest supporter. Your wisdom, patience, and eye for detail helped shape this devotional into something I'm truly proud of. Your unwavering belief in me and in the message God placed in my spirit has been a constant source of strength. Thank you for standing beside me and praying for me.

With all my love and gratitude,
Janai Imani

A Prayer For The Woman Reading This Journal

I thank God for leading you to this devotional. I pray that it not only blesses you, but it transforms you. I pray it helps you become more like Jesus and more like the woman He has destined you to be.

God has a plan for your life and you must learn the tools to carry it out. I pray this devotional equips you with the right tools to walk confidently in your purpose.

I pray that as you become the woman God called you to be, you will be a blessing to those around you, and favor will be poured out on them. I pray God gives you the strength, determination, and grace to go on this journey.

Trust that He has the absolute best for you and that as you walk with Him, you will accomplish all He has set out for you.

In Jesus name, Amen.

Introduction

The Proverbs 31 woman is often held up as the ultimate example of godly womanhood—strong, wise, diligent, and full of grace. She is celebrated as a wife, a mother, and a pillar of her household. As we read this passage, it's important to remember that the essence of the Proverbs 31 woman isn't confined to her roles. Her virtues are timeless and universal, offering valuable lessons for every woman, no matter her journey or the season of life she finds herself in. This devotional invites you to step into her story in a way that applies to your life.

Whether you are single, married, a mother, or navigating life on your own, the principles of the Proverbs 31 woman are qualities we can all strive to cultivate. This devotional isn't about becoming *her* in the literal sense, but about becoming the woman God has called you to be.

Over the next 30 days, we will reflect on the attributes of the Proverbs 31 woman and how they translate into modern life. Together, we will explore what it means to lead with faith, steward our resources well, extend kindness to others, and walk with confidence in the unique calling God has placed on each of our lives.

~ Day 1 ~

The Proverbs 31 woman is a wife of noble character, who is first a woman of noble character. A virtuous woman has high moral standards, and finds her true value in the fabric of her character. The way she treats others, her unwavering trustworthiness, and boundless compassion shape her unforgettable presence in this world.

When you think of the way you show up in your life daily, do you believe you represent this virtuous woman? Well, in this devotional we will be exploring practical ways to apply the principles of Proverbs 31 to your daily life.

Think of three characteristics you believe a virtuous woman has, then think of some ways or habits you can implement in your day to day life to help you get closer to becoming the virtuous woman God created you to be.

Consider the effect your influence has on your family, your community, and your purpose? As a woman of noble character, you have to be committed to personal development so you can better serve those around you.

God, help me to uphold your character and value in my daily life. I know that my purpose requires me to become the best version of myself, so guide me as I strive to fulfill all that you have created me to be. I pray that I will treat others with love and compassion. Father, guide me as I become her, the woman you have called me to be. Amen.

_____

_____

_____

_____

_____

_____

_____

_____

_____

_____

_____

_____

_____

_____

_____

_____

_____

_____

~ Day 2 ~

"Who can find a virtuous and capable wife?
She is more precious than rubies."
Proverbs 31:10

A woman of noble character has a beauty that radiates from within. She has the remarkable inner strength of a ruby, empowering her to face challenges with resilience and grace. She is a rare gem, set apart by her uniqueness and the quality of her character.

When people are blessed to have a woman like this in their lives, they have something more valuable than rubies, riches, or money could ever bring them. Nothing compares to a true woman of God. Proverbs 18:22 says that a man who finds a wife finds a good thing and obtains favor from the Lord. When you focus on being the woman God called you to be in every way, you bring favor to you and those around you.

Reflect on how God has set you apart from others. Oftentimes these traits are closely connected to our purpose. Discovering your purpose requires you to embrace your individuality and unlock the potential within you. What are three characteristics you believe make you unique? Thank God for these today, and consider how they have blessed the people in your life.

God, I ask that as obstacles arise around me you help me to face them with resilience and grace. I pray others will be blessed by the uniqueness you created in me. I pray that my impact outlives the trends of my time, that my character is rooted in you and your word. Father, guide me as I become her, the woman you have called me to be. Amen.

~ Day 3 ~

"Her husband can trust her.
And she will greatly enrich his life."
Proverbs 31:11

G od has designed you to be a woman that adds value to those around you. He knows that if He blesses you, others will be blessed through you. Strive to add value to the people in your life.

This requires you to be a trustworthy woman. Are you a safe place for others? Have you created an environment that can nurture their souls? Life is like a garden filled with beautiful flowers. All flowers start their journey as seeds, so the quality of your garden depends on your ability to create an environment that helps your seeds blossom.

It also requires reliability and accountability. Can people trust your word? Do they believe that you will do what you say you will? Are you disciplined enough to carry out the assignment God has on your life? Reflect on these questions today and consider what your habits and level of discipline say to God and those around you.

God, help me to be a blessing to those around me. I thank you for being my safe place and I pray that I can be a safe place for others to trust me. Help me to be slow to speak and quick to listen. Help me to be mindful of the things I do and say, so that they will have a positive impact on the lives around me. Help me to be disciplined, reliable, and accountable to gracefully walk in my purpose. Father, guide me as I become her, the woman you have called me to be. Amen.

~ Day 4 ~

"She brings him good, not harm, all the days of her life."
Proverbs 31:12

God has called us to be a light unto others and move through the world in love. Each day is another chance to be a blessing to the people we love. A loving woman pours into those around her, helping them become the best versions of themselves.

The work you do and the words you speak should build people up. How do you respond when you are hurting? As a woman, be mindful not to allow your emotions to lead you astray. Acting out of emotion can cause harm to others with your actions or words.

Learning healthy ways to communicate, handle stress, and make it through your bad days can greatly improve the way you interact with others. Think about the way you react on the tough days, are you proud of these habits? Do you believe that's how God would want you to handle them? Think of three healthy ways you can handle the tough days and overwhelming emotions. Lean on these when those times come. Focus on responding and not reacting. Even if your response means to step away and have quiet time with the Lord.

God, help me to be a kind and loving woman even when I'm hurting. Help me to find the beauty within me everyday, even when it's hard. I want the experience people have with me to be positive and filled with love. I know this can only happen with you. Father, guide me as I become her, the woman you have called me to be. Amen.

_____

_____

_____

_____

_____

_____

_____

_____

_____

_____

_____

_____

_____

_____

_____

_____

_____

_____

_____

_____

~ Day 5 ~

"She finds wool and flax and busily spins it."
Proverbs 31:13

A successful woman is a resourceful woman. She embodies adaptability, resilience, and innovation. She refuses to let her circumstances determine her destiny. When faced with obstacles she relies on her creativity and uses the gifts that God has given her to be victorious.

A busy woman isn't always a purposeful woman. Fill your time with meaningful work that enriches both yourself and others. Use your resources to fulfill all that God has created you to be. Remember, you already have everything you need to be the woman God envisioned you to be today, and God will give you everything you need for the woman of tomorrow!

What are some things God has already given you that you may have overlooked or underutilized? We can get so caught up in asking God for more that we don't always appreciate what He has already given us.

God, I want to be a resourceful and purposeful woman. Help me not to focus on my circumstance, but instead who you've created me to be. I know that with you I will be victorious in all things. I thank you that I have every-

thing I need for today, and by faith I believe you will give me everything I need for tomorrow. Father, guide me as I become her, the woman you have called me to be. Amen.

_____

_____

_____

_____

_____

_____

_____

_____

_____

_____

_____

_____

_____

_____

_____

_____

_____

_____

_____

_____

_____

_____

_____

~ Day 6 ~

"She is like a merchant's ship, bringing her food from afar."
Proverbs 31:14

When a noble woman walks in a room, help walks in. She will go to the ends of the earth to make sure her people have what they need. Are you willing to go above and beyond for your purpose?

The reason the Proverbs 31 woman travels so far is because she wants the best for her household. She's not willing to settle for anything less than what she knows they deserve and she can accomplish. She is patient and knows that good things take time. The fastest and easiest options aren't always the best. She's committed to quality and doesn't settle for less.

Are there areas in your life that you know you've settled for less? What do you believe God intended for you to have instead? God is a God who restores. I believe that he will restore everything to you in due time.

God, please give me the strength to go above and beyond for me, my purpose, and those around me. I know you want the best for me and I am committed to going after it, no matter how far or long it takes me. Give me the patience and determination I need to fully accomplish the assignment you've given me. Father, guide me as I become her, the woman you have called me to be. Amen.

~ Day 7 ~

"She gets up before dawn to prepare breakfast for her household and plan the day's work for her servant girls."
Proverbs 31:15

Becoming a woman of noble character is a daily journey. Part of making the most of your day is waking up early. When you're up early, not only does it show your commitment and gratitude to God, but it allows you the time to properly prepare for your day.

Waking early gives you quiet time for yourself and for God to speak to you before the world comes knocking. Oftentimes we are pulled in many directions throughout the day. There's so many people who depend on you and you want to be able to give them your best. But waking early also requires discipline, it may not be easy, but fight the desire to sleep in.

What are a few healthy habits you can incorporate into your morning to develop a solid morning routine? Start little by little and grow as you go. Maybe it's waking up 15 minutes earlier, maybe it's spending 30 minutes of quiet time with God, maybe it's taking a walk outside. Whatever it may be for you, you'll start to notice the impact a good morning routine has on your day, your mood, and your productivity.

God, help me to take charge of my body and my day. Waking up early isn't always the easiest for me, but I know it will set me up for a successful day. Help me to establish good habits that are pleasing to you. Father, guide me as I become her, the woman you have called me to be. Amen.

_____

_____

_____

_____

_____

_____

_____

_____

_____

_____

_____

_____

_____

_____

_____

_____

_____

_____

_____

_____

_____

~ Day 8 ~

A virtuous woman is a woman with a plan. Setting a plan helps you to work through your day with intention and purpose in each thing you do. Being intentional will help you say yes to things God wants you to focus on and say no to things that may distract you from what's important.

It's also important to not be ruled by your plan. You can make all the plans you want, but God has the final say. Invite God into your plans, allow Him to guide you and be open to Him changing the plan. Learn to be adaptable so you can gracefully handle unexpected changes that may come your way without losing your cool.

Do you find making a plan to be challenging? Do you have a hard time accepting change and still feeling confident in your ability to do well? Invite God into this area of your life. He is a God of order and intention, and giving the best to those around us means we have to be intentional about everything we do.

God, help me to be intentional every day. Guide me as I plan my days and help me to accept your will and any changes that may come my way.

I don't want to be taken out of character because of stress or unexpected changes. Give me the peace to be rooted in your word daily, regardless of what life throws at me. Father, guide me as I become her, the woman you have called me to be. Amen.

_____

_____

_____

_____

_____

_____

_____

_____

_____

_____

_____

_____

_____

_____

_____

_____

_____

_____

_____

_____

_____

_____

_____

~ Day 9 ~

"She gets up before dawn to prepare breakfast for her household and plan the day's work for her servant girls."
Proverbs 31:15

Another thing you can learn from this virtuous woman, is knowing when to ask for help. I believe that God strategically places people in your life to help you carry out your purpose. The same way that you are that person in other people's lives. This means you have to accept the help God has provided for you. Sometimes the Proverbs 31 woman can seem like superwoman, but even this amazing woman knew she could not do it all by herself.

You also have to honor the help you have been blessed with. That means leading them well, being graceful and kind to them, and showing gratitude in your words and actions. She took the time to carefully plan the day and be intentional about what she needed help with. She communicated with her servant girls and gave them direction and guidance to make the most of their help.

Do you know how to effectively ask for help, give direction, and trust that they will accomplish it? Sometimes the hardest part of asking for help is trusting someone else will complete the task as well as you know you can. As God gives you more in life, you'll have to learn to relinquish that control and allow others to take on tasks.

Trust in their abilities to perform and your ability to direct them to complete it to God's standard.

God, help me to ask for help. I thank you for the people and resources you've given me. I ask that you help me to steward them well. I pray for communication that is clear and kind, I pray for patience and trust. I know I can't accomplish everything on my own, help me to lean on my village and have faith. Father, guide me as I become her, the woman you have called me to be. Amen.

_____

_____

_____

_____

_____

_____

_____

_____

_____

_____

_____

_____

_____

_____

_____

_____

_____

~ Day 10 ~

*"She goes to inspect a field and buys it; with her
earnings she plants a vineyard."*
Proverbs 31:16

This woman exercised wise judgment. Not only did she recognize a good opportunity when it was presented to her, but she also understood the importance of patience, avoiding hasty decisions, and choosing wisely. She was willing to step out of her comfort zone and receive what God was offering her. Sometimes, all God asks for is your effort and willingness.

She understood that not everything that glitters is gold, which is why she took the time to inspect the field before making the investment. Just because something looks good on the surface doesn't mean it's what God has planned for you. Allow God to guide you as you make decisions for yourself and your household.

Reflect on how you approach opportunities. Do you pause to seek God's guidance and carefully evaluate situations? Consider times when being patient led to better outcomes in your life, and how hasty decisions may have caused challenges. Before taking any significant step, spend time in prayer, asking God for wisdom and clarity. Measure every opportunity against biblical principles.

If something aligns with God's truth, it's worth considering; if not, it may be a distraction.

God, I invite you into my decision making. Help me to be wise and intentional in every decision I make. Help me to recognize good opportunities and help me to manage them well. Help me to exercise faith and courage to invest in opportunities that can change lives. Guide me through the decision making process and help me to be patient. Father, guide me as I become her, the woman you have called me to be. Amen.

_____

_____

_____

_____

_____

_____

_____

_____

_____

_____

_____

_____

_____

_____

_____

_____

_____

_____

~ Day 11 ~

*"She goes to inspect a field and buys it; with her earnings
she plants a vineyard."*
Proverbs 31:16

Not only did this woman make smart investment, she managed her earnings well. Don't be frivolous with the blessings God gives you. Be intentional and wise to make the most of what He's given you. Women have a unique ability to multiply what they've been given.

As a woman, it can feel easy to act on your impulses or treat yourself to your heart's desire. However, you need to be prudent and exercise wisdom when it comes to your spending habits. If you spend wisely, you can multiply your income and be blessed with more. This means denying instant gratification and patiently watching your money grow and work for you.

Reflect on how you manage the resources God has entrusted to you. Are you using them with intention and wisdom, or are you being careless or impulsive? Develop a spending plan that prioritizes essentials, savings, and investments. Ensure that your spending aligns with your values and goals. Read books, take courses, or listen to podcasts about personal finance to increase your knowledge and confidence.

God, give me the wisdom to multiply the blessings you give me. Help me to be patient and wise in what I choose to spend my money on. Help me to not be ruled by money, but to use it to my advantage. Show me the best ways to manage my finances, so I can do more to glorify your kingdom. Father, guide me as I become her, the woman you have called me to be. Amen.

~ Day 12 ~

*"She is energetic and strong, a hard worker. She makes sure
her dealings are profitable; her lamp burns late into the night."*
Proverbs 31:17-18

A virtuous woman works hard and puts her best effort into everything she does. Hard work is important, but maintaining a joyful spirit while working can be even more challenging. Finding joy in the little things helps cultivate gratitude and gives you the strength to endure when the journey gets tough. She doesn't worry about how long it may take—she trusts that if God started a good work in her, He will see it through to completion. (Philippians 1:6)

Being a hard worker isn't just about effort; it's also about working smart. Knowing where to focus your energy and recognizing when to seek help in areas outside your expertise will propel you forward while preserving your peace and sanity. When challenges arise, remember that God has uniquely created you for your purpose. With Him at the center, you will accomplish all that He has planned for you.

Start each day by listing three things you're grateful for in your work or life. This habit can help you find joy even in small, mundane tasks. In what areas of your life do you tend to "disqualify" yourself? These areas could be exactly where God is positioning you to create change and glorify Him. Remind yourself of God's promises when difficulties arise. Keep verses or affirmations handy that encourage you to stay resilient and trust in His plan.

God, I ask that you be my strength in this process. I recognize that I can't do this alone, and I thank you for walking with me. Help me to experience joy in the little things and remember that I'm doing it all for your glory. Father, guide me as I become her, the woman you have called me to be. Amen.

~ Day 13 ~

"Her hands are busy spinning thread,
her fingers twisting fiber."
Proverbs 31:19

Everyone has a unique gift. Although the Proverbs 31 woman had help, she wasn't afraid to get her hands dirty and dive into the work. She focused on what she was good at—and perhaps what she enjoyed most. You don't have to be superwoman and do everything yourself. Allow God to guide you in discerning what to handle personally and when to enlist help.

The Bible warns against idleness and laziness, and we can learn from the Proverbs 31 woman's work ethic. She doesn't work all day, every day—she knows when to rest. She uses her time wisely, is productive and resourceful. Becoming the woman God has called you to be requires discipline, especially during moments when inspiration and motivation are lacking.

What habits or routines can you implement to avoid idleness and stay disciplined, even when motivation is low? Make a list of three things you want to commit to, and reflect on the challenges that have kept you from completing them. Consider how discipline can help you overcome these obstacles.

God, help me not to be idle, but to faithfully work for Your glory each day. Teach me to stay disciplined even when my motivation fades. Help me to be productive while allowing time for rest. You said the weary can come to You, and You will give them rest (Matthew 11:28 NLT). I know the best rest is found in You, so I trust that working with You and for You will sustain me. Father, guide me as I become the woman You have called me to be. Amen.

_____

_____

_____

_____

_____

_____

_____

_____

_____

_____

_____

_____

_____

_____

_____

_____

_____

_____

_____

~ Day 14 ~

"She extends a helping hand to the poor
and opens her arms to the needy."
Proverbs 31:20

God blesses you not just for your own benefit, but so you can be a blessing to those around you. His generosity flows through you, allowing you to meet the needs of others. When you encounter someone in need, don't turn away—ask God for the resources, wisdom, and creativity to help. Helping others isn't a one-size-fits-all approach; your unique gifts and talents are part of God's design for serving others.

Think of the Proverbs 31 woman—perhaps she made clothes for the poor or shared goods from the merchant ships. She used what was available to her. With God, even the smallest acts of kindness can have a profound impact. A little goes a long way in His hands. So even if you feel like what you have to offer isn't enough, trust God to multiply it.

Think about a woman you admire—someone who uses her gifts to uplift and serve others. What is it about her that inspires you? Is it her generosity, her confidence in using what she has, or the way she seems to notice the needs around her? Reflect on how her actions have impacted you or others. Could you see yourself stepping into a similar role, using the gifts God has placed in you to make a difference?

God, thank You for Your continuous blessings and favor in my life. Help me to see these blessings not as something to hold onto, but to pour into others. Show me creative ways to use my gifts to serve and build Your kingdom. Open my eyes to the problems I was uniquely designed to solve. Give me the courage and compassion to step forward, and trust that even when I feel inadequate, with you all things are possible. Father, guide me as I become the woman You have called me to be. Amen.

_____
_____
_____
_____
_____
_____
_____
_____
_____
_____
_____
_____
_____
_____
_____
_____
_____
_____
_____

~ Day 15 ~

"She has no fear of winter for her household,
for everyone has warm clothes."
Proverbs 31:21

The Proverbs 31 woman didn't wait for winter to arrive—her family was already clothed and ready for the cold. She used wisdom and foresight to prepare, ensuring that they lacked nothing when the season changed. Sometimes, God gives you more than you need in a particular season, and you may wonder why, but God knows the path ahead. What may seem unnecessary now could be exactly what you'll need in the future. His provision often arrives before the need, and part of walking in faith is trusting His timing and purpose.

As you navigate the different seasons, seek God's guidance on how to use the resources He's given you. It's easy to overspend, over-commit, or overlook what we have when things seem abundant. But wisdom allows us to manage those blessings carefully, ensuring that we're not left unprepared when circumstances shift.

Think about the areas in your life where you feel unprepared for unexpected challenges. Are there parts of your household, finances, or spiritual life that could use more intentional planning or organization? What steps can you take today to build a system that helps you feel more prepared for whatever lies ahead? Sometimes, the breakthrough isn't in asking for more, but in managing well what you already have.

God, thank You for being my provider and for blessing me in ways I sometimes don't even recognize. Help me to not see the extra You've given me as coincidence but as preparation for the days ahead. Give me the wisdom to manage my resources well and the discernment to know when to save, when to give, and when to step out in faith. Teach me to trust in Your timing and not to fear the future, knowing that You go before me. Father, guide me as I become the woman You have called me to be. Amen.

~ Day 16 ~

"She makes her own bedspreads. She dresses in
fine linen and purple gowns."
Proverbs 31:22

As women, it's easy to get caught up in serving and caring for others. While giving is part of our nature, we often forget to care for ourselves in the process. But remember this: you can't pour from an empty cup. God wants to fill your heart, renew your spirit, and remind you that you deserve rest, love, and joy. When you allow Him to fill you, you're able to show up as the best version of yourself—for you and for the people around you.

Carrying yourself with dignity and grace is an extension of the love you show yourself. Take pride in the way you present yourself to the world, not for approval but as a reflection of the beauty God placed within you. When you look good, you feel good—it's a simple yet powerful reminder to honor yourself. Give yourself the time, care, and attention you so freely give to others. You are worthy of a life that feels rich in quality, love, and peace.

How are you currently prioritizing self-care and personal growth in your daily life? Are there areas that feel overlooked or neglected? If so, what's holding you back from making yourself a priority? Think of two small but meaningful ways you can begin pouring into yourself. Maybe it's something as simple as a walk in nature, a quiet moment with a cup of tea, or diving into a new book.

God, thank You for the reminder that I am worthy of care, rest, and love. Help me to slow down and make time to nourish my body, mind, and soul. Fill my heart with Your peace and joy, and lead me to the places where I can find true rest in You. Restore me so that I can care for others from a place of fullness. Father, guide me as I become her, the woman you have called me to be. Amen.

_____

_____

_____

_____

_____

_____

_____

_____

_____

_____

_____

_____

_____

_____

_____

_____

_____

~ Day 17 ~

*"Her husband is well known at the city gates, where he sits
with the other civic leaders."*
Proverbs 31:23

The people you surround yourself with play a significant role in shaping your journey. Having the right circle doesn't just provide emotional support—it can open doors, offer guidance, and help you navigate life's relationships with grace and wisdom. The Proverbs 31 woman likely benefited from her husband's reputation and influence. His leadership and standing at the city gates may have strengthened her connections with merchants, inspired loyalty among her servant girls, or motivated her to uphold her own high standards of work and character.

When God blesses you with the right relationships—what I like to call *purpose partners*—it's a sign of His divine alignment. These connections aren't by chance; they are designed to propel you forward in your calling. You aren't meant to walk this path alone. God often places people in your life whose gifts, strengths, and experiences complement your own, creating a support system that helps you thrive.

Take a moment to reflect on your inner circle. Who are the people that uplift, challenge, and inspire you? Are there relationships that encourage your growth and keep you accountable? On the other hand, are there any connections that may be holding you back or draining your energy? Ask God to reveal the purpose behind your current relationships and to align you with individuals who will pour into your life as you pour into others.

God, thank You for the people You've placed in my life. I am grateful for the relationships that bring encouragement, wisdom, and joy. Lord, help me to clearly see who You have called to walk alongside me in this season. Align me with purpose partners who will uplift and challenge me, and allow me to be a source of strength and support for them as well. Show me how to nurture these connections with grace and love. Father, guide me as I become her, the woman you have called me to be. Amen.

_____

_____

_____

_____

_____

_____

_____

_____

_____

_____

_____

_____

_____

_____

~ Day 18 ~

"She makes belted linen garments and
sashes to sell to the merchants."
Proverbs 31:24

As Christians, it's easy to feel torn between generosity and profitability. Sometimes, in the desire to help others, we undervalue our own abilities—giving freely but hesitating to charge for our services or talents. While kindness and generosity are beautiful reflections of God's heart, God desires for you to thrive, to create wealth that sustains your family, and to be a source of blessing to your community. By fully embracing and maximizing your gifts, you allow Him to multiply your impact. This doesn't diminish your compassion; it empowers you to give even more from a place of abundance.

At the same time, not every skill or talent needs to be monetized. Some gifts are meant to simply bring joy, provide peace, or deepen your relationship with God. A hobby, a creative outlet, or an act of service can glorify God just as much as a profitable business venture. The key is finding balance—and God is the best guide to help you discern when to give freely and when to use your talents for profit. Trust that He will show you how to walk in both generosity and prosperity.

What hobbies or talents bring you joy but don't necessarily need to be turned into a source of income? How can you allow yourself to enjoy them without pressure? Ask God for clarity and wisdom—where is He leading you to maximize your gifts, and where is He inviting you to rest and simply enjoy them?

God, help me to see the value in what I offer and to embrace the opportunities You provide for me to thrive. Teach me to steward my skills well. Let me find joy in the simple, creative things that bring me closer to You. Give me discernment to know when to give freely and when to step confidently into profitability. May all that I do reflect Your glory and align with the purpose You have for my life. Father, guide me as I become her, the woman you have called me to be. Amen.

_____

_____

_____

_____

_____

_____

_____

_____

_____

_____

_____

_____

_____

_____

~ Day 19 ~

"She is clothed with strength and dignity, and she
laughs without fear of the future."
Proverbs 31:25

Be strong and courageous. There's no need to worry about the future—God is not only with you but has already gone ahead of you and paved the way. The path before you is no accident; it's been carefully and beautifully curated to bless you, challenge you, and shape you into the extraordinary woman He created you to be. With God by your side, there is nothing you can't handle. When obstacles arise, don't shrink back—stand firm, put on the armor of God, and face each challenge with boldness and grace.

God's desire is for you to live with joy and peace, regardless of your circumstances. This doesn't mean life will always be smooth sailing—storms will come, but so will His steady hand to guide you through. By anchoring your faith in Him, you'll find the strength to endure, and you'll emerge stronger, wiser, and more refined than when you began.

It's easy to shy away when things get tough, but can you recall a time when you faced something head-on and felt God carrying you through? Maybe it didn't feel like it in the moment, but looking back, you can see His hand in it. Now, consider the areas of your life where you feel most uncertain about the future. Is it your career, relationships, or maybe just the unknown of what's next? What would it look like to fully trust that God has already gone ahead of you, preparing the way even if you can't see it yet?

God, thank You for walking beside me and going before me. I am grateful that I never have to face life's challenges alone. When I feel weak or afraid, remind me of Your constant presence and unfailing love. Help me to be strong and courageous, trusting that You have equipped me to handle whatever comes my way. Fill my heart with peace and joy, even in uncertain times. Let me find rest in the knowledge that You are always working things out for my good. Father, guide me as I become her, the woman you have called me to be. Amen.

~ Day 20 ~

"When she speaks, her words are wise, and she
gives instructions with kindness."
Proverbs 31:26

E ducating yourself and seeking wisdom is essential, but don't let intellect harden your heart. True leadership isn't just about being knowledgeable or decisive—it's about balancing strength with kindness. A good leader listens, shows empathy, and leads with love, while still being firm and effective. The Proverbs 31 woman was respected by her family, children, and even her servants—not because she ruled with an iron fist, but because her actions and words reflected care and love. People follow those they trust, and trust is built through compassion and consistency.

This kind of leadership takes thought and intentional. Before she spoke, she considered not just what she wanted to say, but how her words would impact others. She understood the importance of tailoring her communication to the individual—knowing that what works for one person may not resonate with another. Communication isn't a one-size-fits-all deal, and learning to adapt your approach can transform your relationships and expand your influence.

Think about a time when you had to have a tough conversation. How did you handle it? Were you able to balance honesty with kindness, or do you feel like your words came out harsher (or softer) than intended? It happens to all of us! The important thing is recognizing those moments and learning from them. Imagine how much smoother your conversations could go if you intentionally meet people where they are, speaking in a way they could best receive.

God, I want to lead with love, just as the Proverbs 31 woman did. Teach me to be intentional with my words and to communicate with kindness, compassion, and wisdom. When I'm frustrated or unsure, help me to pause and seek Your guidance before I speak. Let my words reflect Your love and build trust in the hearts of those around me. Father, guide me as I become her, the woman you have called me to be. Amen.

_____
_____
_____
_____
_____
_____
_____
_____
_____
_____
_____
_____
_____
_____
_____

~ Day 21 ~

*"She carefully watches everything in her household
and suffers nothing from laziness."*
Proverbs 31:27

It's easy to overlook the little things when life feels overwhelming. Whether it's rushing through tasks, cutting corners, or letting responsibilities pile up—when you're overworked, the details are often the first to slip through the cracks. But here's the truth: *God is in the details.* The way you handle the small things is reflected in the bigger picture.

This is where self-care and balance come in. When you pour into yourself—getting the rest you need, staying grounded in prayer, and knowing when to ask for help—you'll find it easier to stay sharp and attentive. Being well-rested and spiritually filled doesn't just help you feel better; it allows you to be more present and engaged in your work, relationships, and calling.

Let your love for Jesus and your desire to grow as a godly woman drive you to excellence. Discipline isn't just about doing more; it's about doing the *right things* with intention and care. When your heart is aligned with Him, even the smallest tasks can become acts of worship.

When you start feeling overwhelmed, how do you typically respond? Do you push through and overextend yourself, or do you allow things to slide, hoping to catch up later? We've all been there, so there's no shame in it. But consider this: how different would your days feel if you paused to rest and recharge before the exhaustion set in? What's one small change you can make this week to approach those areas with more care and attention?

God, thank You for reminding me that even the smallest details matter to You. When I feel like cutting corners, guide me back to a place of discipline and peace. Let my work reflect the love I have for You, and may even the simplest tasks bring glory to Your name. Lord, I want to be a woman who approaches every aspect of life with intention, care, and grace. Father, guide me as I become her, the woman you have called me to be. Amen.

_____

_____

_____

_____

_____

_____

_____

_____

_____

_____

_____

_____

_____

_____

~ Day 22 ~

"Her children stand and bless her. Her husband praises her:
"There are many virtuous and capable women in the world, but
you surpass them all!""
Proverbs 31:28-29

The love, wisdom, and values you pour into others—whether your children, family, or those you mentor—create a ripple effect that lasts for generations. What you instill today becomes part of the legacy you leave behind. When your life reflects God's word, the seeds you plant will continue to grow long after you're gone.

But let's be real—pouring into others can feel exhausting, especially when it feels like no one notices the effort you put in. Sometimes, we just need a little appreciation. It's not about grand gestures; even a simple "thank you" or acknowledgment can breathe life into weary hearts. If you've been feeling unseen or undervalued, take a moment to reflect. Who in your life shows appreciation in ways that speak to your heart?

This week, pay attention to the small ways people show love—maybe it's through their actions rather than words. If their way of appreciating you aligns with what you need, take a moment to thank them. But if you feel like your needs aren't being met, don't be afraid to gently communicate that. Let them know how much you love and enjoy serving them, but sometimes, you just need a little acknowledgment too.

Now consider this—how do *you* show appreciation to others? Sometimes, the best way to receive love is to model it. What's one thing you can do this week to let someone know you see and appreciate them?

God, I ask for strength and patience when the work feels heavy, and for moments of rest when I need to recharge. Open my eyes to see the small ways those around me show love and appreciation, even if it looks different from what I expect. And when I feel unseen, remind me that You see every act of love I give. Father, guide me as I become her, the woman you have called me to be. Amen.

_____

_____

_____

_____

_____

_____

_____

_____

_____

_____

_____

_____

_____

_____

~ Day 23 ~

*"Charm is deceptive, and beauty does not last; but a woman
who fears the Lord will be greatly praised."*
Proverbs 31:30

C harm can grab attention, and beauty may turn heads, but neither can sustain the depth of who you truly are. Outward beauty fades with time, but your heart—your character—is what leaves a lasting impact. People may not always remember the dress you wore or how perfectly styled your hair was, but they will remember how you treated them, how you made them feel, and the light you carried within you.

God cares more about the condition of your heart than the image you present to the world. It's not that looking good or presenting yourself well doesn't matter—there's nothing wrong with wanting to look and feel beautiful—but it should never be the foundation of your confidence or self-worth. True beauty shines from a spirit deeply connected to God, reflecting His love, kindness, and grace.

Have you ever caught yourself relying a little too much on appearance or charm to make an impression? It's easy to fall into that pattern, especially in a world that celebrates surface-level beauty. But take a moment and think—who are the people you admire most? Chances are, it's their kindness, wisdom, or strength of character that draws you in, not just how they look. Invite God to shift your focus inward, what's one way you can cultivate the kind of beauty that lasts?

God, thank You for creating me in Your image. Help me to remember that my worth is not tied to how I look but to who I am in You. Teach me to cultivate the kind of beauty that never fades—the beauty of a kind heart, a wise spirit, and a love that reflects Yours. Father, guide me as I become her, the woman you have called me to be. Amen.

~ Day 24 ~

*"Reward her for all she has done. Let her deeds
publicly declare her praise."*
Proverbs 31:31

E very ounce of effort you pour into the work God has placed before you is seen and valued—by Him, even when it feels like no
one else notices. The long hours, the sacrifices, the behind-the-
scenes moments that go unrecognized by the world—God sees it all.
And He promises that none of it is in vain.

Sometimes it feels discouraging when you don't see the fruits of
your labor right away. You might wonder if what you're doing really
matters or if it will ever pay off. But remember this: God is faithful.
The seeds you plant today will bloom in their season. One day, not
only will you feel the weight of His reward, but the world will recognize the treasure that you are.

Have you ever felt like the work you're doing goes unnoticed?
It's easy to feel discouraged when the results aren't immediate. But
take a step back—think of the times in your life when you stayed the
course, even without recognition. What did you learn through that
process? How did God show up for you, even in small ways?

God, thank You for the reminder that nothing I do for You is ever wasted. Strengthen my heart when I feel discouraged and remind me that You see every detail, every sacrifice, and every effort. Help me to rest in the assurance that You will reward the work done in Your name. Father, guide me as I become her, the woman you have called me to be. Amen.

_____

_____

_____

_____

_____

_____

_____

_____

_____

_____

_____

_____

_____

_____

_____

_____

_____

_____

_____

_____

~ Day 25 ~

*"Let us not become weary in doing good, for at the proper
time we will reap a harvest if we do not give up."*
Galatians 6:9

Take a moment to pause and acknowledge how far you've come. Over the past few weeks, you've committed to growing spiritually, emotionally, and mentally. That's no small thing. Whether the journey has felt smooth or challenging, you've taken steps toward becoming the woman God has called you to be. And here's the beautiful part—*growth is continuous.* It doesn't stop at the end of this devotional.

As we enter the final days, we'll shift our focus to something vital—creating a sustainable plan to help you *live out* what you've learned. The goal isn't perfection; it's progress. Real transformation doesn't happen overnight. It happens in the small, consistent steps you take each day. And trust me, those little steps add up to big changes.

How are you feeling about the progress you've made? Take a breath and give yourself credit for showing up, even on the days it felt hard. What's one area where you've noticed growth—big or small? Maybe it's the way you approach prayer, how you speak to others, or simply the peace you feel in your heart.

God, thank You for walking with me through this journey of growth and transformation. I acknowledge the work You've done in my heart, and I am grateful for every lesson learned along the way. Remind me that small steps matter and that progress, not perfection, is what You desire. Father, guide me as I become her, the woman you have called me to be. Amen.

_____

_____

_____

_____

_____

_____

_____

_____

_____

_____

_____

_____

_____

_____

_____

_____

_____

_____

_____

~ Day 26 ~

"Let your eyes look straight ahead; fix your gaze directly be-
fore you. Give careful thought to the paths for your feet and be
steadfast in all your ways."
Proverbs 4:25-26

Review your notes or journal entries from the past few weeks.
What habits, lessons, or character traits consistently spoke to
your heart? Were there certain themes that God kept bringing to
your attention? Take your time with this reflection. If you're not
sure why a certain habit stands out, bring it to God in prayer and
ask for clarity.

Highlight the top 3-5 habits or traits that resonated the
most—these are often the areas where God is nudging you to grow,
strengthen, or embrace more fully. Reflect not only on what stood
out but *why* these particular qualities caught your attention. Maybe
it's something you feel God is already developing within you, or
perhaps it's an area you've been longing to improve.

Reflection Space:
Habit/Character Trait 1: _____
Habit/Character Trait 2: _____
Habit/Character Trait 3: _____

God, as I reflect on the lessons You've shown me, I ask for clarity and wisdom. Reveal the areas where You are calling me to grow and give me the grace to take small, steady steps toward becoming the woman You've created me to be. Help me to stay focused on what truly matters, and let Your word guide my decisions and actions. Father, guide me as I become her, the woman you have called me to be. Amen.

~ Day 27 ~

"Do not despise these small beginnings, for the Lord
rejoices to see the work begin."
Zechariah 4:10

R eflection is powerful, but lasting transformation happens when
we take small, intentional steps. Now that you've identified the
habits or traits God is highlighting in your life, it's time to break
them down into *real, achievable goals.* The key is to start small, as
growth is sustainable when it happens gradually.

Think of one small, measurable action you can take daily or
weekly for each habit. The goal isn't to overwhelm yourself but
to create a rhythm that allows these habits to take root naturally.
Maybe it's waking up 30 minutes earlier for quiet time, dedicating
one evening to journaling, or committing to speak words of encouragement to someone once a day. Even the smallest adjustments,
when done consistently, lead to significant change over time.

Example: If "rising early" resonated, set a goal to wake up 30 minutes
earlier for quiet time or prayer.

Goal-Setting Template:

Habit 1: _____

Goal: _____

Frequency: _____

Habit 2: _____

Goal: _____

Frequency: _____

Habit 3: _____

Goal: _____

Frequency: _____

God, I know that transformation doesn't happen overnight, but I trust that the small steps I take today will lead to lasting change. Help me to set goals that reflect Your purpose for my life, and give me the strength to stay consistent, even when progress feels slow. Let me find joy in the process and peace in knowing that You celebrate every effort, no matter how small. Father, guide me as I become her, the woman you have called me to be. Amen.

_____

_____

_____

_____

_____

_____

_____

_____

_____

_____

_____

~ Day 28 ~

As you begin to implement the habits and traits God is highlighting in your life, it's important to recognize that challenges will arise. Life gets busy, unexpected circumstances pop up, and sometimes motivation fades. That's normal. But identifying potential obstacles ahead of time allows you to prepare and stay grounded when distractions come.

Take a moment to think about what might hinder you from consistently practicing these new habits. Is it time management, lack of energy, or simply forgetting to prioritize them? By anticipating these roadblocks, you can brainstorm solutions that fit your lifestyle and keep you moving forward. Remember, God doesn't expect perfection—He desires persistence and a willingness to grow.

Example: *Goal: Growing Spiritually*

Challenge: Feeling too tired at the end of the day.
Solution: Shift your quiet time to the morning or during lunch breaks when your mind is fresh.

Obstacle/ Solution Space:

Habit 1 Challenge: _____
Solution: _____

Habit 2 Challenge: _____
Solution: _____

Habit 3 Challenge: _____
Solution: _____

God, I know that walking in these habits will draw me closer to You. Help me to see obstacles not as setbacks, but as opportunities to lean on You for strength and guidance. Show me creative solutions and fill me with the perseverance to stay committed, even when it feels difficult. Father, guide me as I become her, the woman you have called me to be. Amen.

_____
_____
_____
_____
_____
_____
_____
_____
_____
_____
_____

~ Day 29 ~

"Commit to the Lord whatever you do,
and he will establish your plans."
Proverbs 16:3

Building new habits is easier when you have a plan that fits into your daily life. By drafting a simple routine, you create space for the habits and character traits you want to develop. The goal isn't to pack your day with tasks, but to create a rhythm that allows you to grow consistently without feeling overwhelmed. Keep it flexible—life happens, and routines should adapt to the seasons you're in. The key is *intention.*

Think about the flow of your day. Are your mornings quiet and peaceful, or do you find more focus in the evenings? Align your habits with the times when you naturally feel most present and energized.

Example: Morning - Prayer and Scripture Reading (20 minutes)
Evening - Reflect on one positive act of kindness.

Template:
Morning: _____
Afternoon: _____
Evening: _____

God, I desire to honor You with my time and establish habits that draw me closer to You. Help me to create a routine that reflects my heart's desire to grow, but give me the grace to remain flexible when life feels unpredictable. Father, guide me as I become her, the woman you have called me to be. Amen.

~ Day 30 ~

"Two are better than one, because they have a good return
for their labor: If either of them falls down,
one can help the other up."
Ecclesiastes 4:9-10

As you reach the final day of this devotional, I want to encourage you not to take this journey alone. Growth flourishes in community, and having someone to walk alongside you can make all the difference. Whether it's a friend, mentor, spouse, or family member, find someone you trust who can encourage you, pray with you, and keep you accountable as you continue to grow in the habits and lessons you've developed.

Accountability isn't about perfection or pressure—it's about having someone who gently reminds you of your goals and speaks life into you when motivation fades. We all need people who can lift us up, challenge us to stay the course, and celebrate the victories, no matter how small.

Take a moment to reflect on the people in your life. Who naturally encourages you? Who do you feel safe sharing your goals and struggles with? This person doesn't need to have everything figured out—they just need to be someone who loves you and is willing to grow alongside you.

Pray for God to reveal the right accountability partner. Sometimes the best person isn't who we initially think. Let God lead you to the person who will uplift and inspire you.

Reach out. Send a text or make a call—invite someone to join you on this journey. Explain what you're working on and ask if they'd be willing to check in with you regularly.

Be intentional. Set small goals together, schedule check-ins, and encourage each other often. Relationships thrive when nurtured with consistency.

_____

_____

_____

_____

_____

_____

_____

_____

_____

_____

_____

_____

_____

_____

_____

_____

About The Author

Janai Imani, the visionary behind Black Girl Bible, is a passionate advocate for empowering young women through faith. As a young black woman herself, Janai has experienced firsthand the unique challenges that come with navigating society. She created Black Girl Bible to provide a safe and inspiring space where young women can grow spiritually, find their purpose, and strengthen their relationship with God.

With a Bachelor of Arts in Psychology and a Master of Business Administration, Janai combines her academic background with her passion for inspiring others. A first-generation Jamaican American originally from New York, she now resides in Atlanta, where she continues to uplift and empower others.

Through her podcast, Janai shares her personal journey, offering Godly advice rooted in the Bible on how to overcome obstacles, build self-worth, and live a life that honors God. Her authentic and relatable approach resonates deeply with her audience, encouraging them to embrace their identity in Christ and walk confidently in their calling.